THE

ABC's

of YOUTH
MINISTRY
LEADERSHIP

Actions that Bridge Lasting Connections

TAKEITHA PETERSON CARTER

Book Cover Design: Prize Publishing House

Printed by: Prize Publishing House, LLC in the United States of Americ

First printing edition 2025.

Prize Publishing House
P.O. Box 9856, Chesapeake, VA 23321
www.PrizePublishingHouse.com

ISBN (Paperback): 979-8-9925617-7-7
ISBN (E-Book): 979-8-9925617-8-4

Letter of Dedication to
My Beloved Mentor & Angel

For believing in me as a Youth Ministry Leader and change agent in this space, this book is dedicated to the memory of the late Joyce L. Rodgers, Youth Ministry Leader par excellent. Your commitment to my transformation, acceptance of my voice, and authentic creativity, which continue to lead me to my destiny, are stamped in my heart. Many times I felt as though I "failed;" however, during those times, you reminded me that I was being *"formed."* Thus, to your credit, my wings are spreading.

With each opportunity, I feel the thrust of your trust. It's the strong whisper of your confidence in my ability, the positive nod of your head peeking from the side of the stage, and the heavy winds of your anointed prayers that often would catch me when I did not even know I was falling. Often, your calls would leave me in tears, as you would call just to speak life, applaud, and pray. You would hang up after that ministry moment without saying "goodbye," and this is the quiet way you left. Most of us share the sentiment of you slipping away without notice – without an official "goodbye." Yet, your classic, intentional mini-boot camps prepared us for every facet of ministry transitions – including yours, the day you became one of heaven's most Glorious Angels.

You challenged me, having you as my blanket of comfort with the acceptance of your eternal crown – the most befitting adornment for the ultimate Young Woman of Excellence. Therefore, as I continue to navigate this unique journey of leadership, encapsulated with smiles and tears, it is with gratitude that I humbly submit my appreciation to you for snatching me from the bonds of insignificance and the backdrop of obscurity, granting me the chance to glean from the never-ending wells of your heart.

Because of you, today, I stand on my own two feet as a product of your time, your training, your patience, your discipline, your celebrations, and most of all, your prayers. I am so happy that I was able to share with you on numerous occasions that what you instilled within me privately took root and blossomed publicly, both in church and in the corporate sector. I am now a portal for energy and information delivered in the fashion in which you taught.

Sleep on, mighty Feminine Warrior. Rest in power, Giant Slayer. Your physical presence is absent, but your spiritual imprint is felt and ever-present. I love you ALWAYS...

You will always be our #SafetyPinGirl and my #ForeverChairlady.

Takeitha Peterson Carter
Assistant Chairlady, International Youth and Young Adult Department
Church Of God In Christ, Inc.

CONTENTS

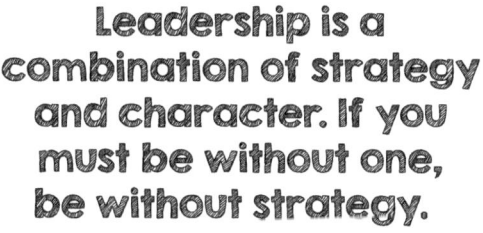

Leadership is a
combination of strategy
and character. If you
must be without one,
be without strategy.

GENERAL H. NORMAN SCHWARZKOPE

FOREWORD

Youth ministry, in my opinion, is truly a misunderstood field. You've got one camp that thinks youth leaders don't do anything but hand out pizza and play musical chairs and another camp that thinks we are extreme, putting undue pressure on the kids to be committed to Jesus before they've gotten a chance to live life. Most leaders actually exist somewhere in the middle of the two extremes. We do whatever is necessary to help the kids that show up. We feed them because *they need food*. We play with them because *they are kids*. We minister to them because *that encompasses our role as leaders in youth ministry*.

Youth Leaders do all of this and so much more. Many of us are the "second parents" to young people; as Youth Leaders are the ones who have to have the tough conversations about sexuality and gender identity; about religion and faith; about domestic abuse and healthy relationships; about peer pressure and bullying; about LIFE – before ever speaking to their biological parents surrounding these issues. Young people look to us for advice to walk through life, and we are expected to have answers.

Youth ministry is fluid because it has to meet the needs of the church demographic that is constantly changing. Young people are growing, developing, learning, and becoming – and it is the Youth Leader's job to walk them through all of it. We do this while navigating the often-conflicting demands of parents and church leaders and the (often unhelpful) influences of TikTok and Instagram.

Are you overwhelmed yet?

Yes?

Then you need this relevant and refreshing content.

My dear sister has managed to break this overwhelming calling down into the basics. We don't have to be everything all the time to everyone. God designed this thing to be much simpler than what it has morphed into over the years.

So, take a breath, take a beat, and digest the simplicity of what youth ministry could be.

Chairlady Seantea J. Stewart
Southern California Second Jurisdiction
Youth Ministry Leader

CHAPTER

1

HOW DID YOU SHOW UP?

Let's start here. Imagine this. Youth Ministry. New Century. You are the Youth Leader who has set out to connect youth to youth ministry. You've watched other youth groups, and you have seen the outcome that events have had on young people. You put in your mind that you are going to "try it," and you open an opportunity for the youth to meet you at the skating rink.

You are there amongst the hustle and bustle of helping young people check-in, tying up skates, and waving bye to the parents who dropped off their kids so that they can enjoy time to themselves. You answer the tap on your shoulder and give your smiling consent to a group of young people asking to go over to the concession area while simultaneously speaking with other Youth Leaders and sharing the event assignments with the team.

The music is blasting, young people are laughing, and everyone is having a ball. YET, there is ONE problem. YOU are all dressed up in your Sunday best, with no real intention to skate. You are watching from the sidelines, and although you are stationed at the rink, you look ready for a good Bible lesson that will be followed by an awesome worship experience.

While young people can appreciate the fact that you have offered something fun, their ability to connect with you is diminished by how you showed up! YOU invited them into a space of fun, relaxation, and comfort, all to silently disconnect them by your appearance and inability to participate and truly connect.

Hello! It's nice to meet you! My name is Takeitha Peterson Carter, and I am a Youth Ministry Strategist. That's right! A part of my God-given assignment is connecting Youth Leaders to Youth Ministry, encouraging, empowering, and equipping them for Youth Ministry Leadership – and I absolutely enjoy doing just that!

Now let's walk back to the skating rink. Why was that scenario so important? Well, it simply sets the stage for HOW YOU SHOW UP as a Youth Leader. Not just at the skating rink but how you show up in the lives of the young people that God will allow you to influence – be it through events, gatherings, rehearsals, church services, graduations, Zoom calls, or social media posts.

Everything thrives – or dies – on how you "show up" as a Youth Leader. Take an introspective assessment: What does the reflection of your influence look like? Les Brown says, "It's impossible to see the picture when you are in the frame." What will the generations proclaim about you when you move out of the frame? Are you intimidated by youthful talent and vibrant beauty? Are you afraid to address questions that are relevant? Do you openly embrace differences and address them with the love of Jesus Christ? Are you quick to rebuke before building a solid relationship? Are you impartial? Can you disciple and discipline simultaneously? Are you the grave of the ministry you are leading? Will all you have to offer be a grave? Will your bones rest on a generation that you killed or that you built?

> **Influence is not about a denomination. It is about your ability to impact the life of another.**
>
> TAKEITHA PETERSON CARTER

The fact that you are responsible for the lives who are watching your every move is important. Young people hang on your every word because they view you as the mouthpiece of righteousness. They rarely disregard your premise, especially if there is a genuine relationship. Therefore, you do not have time to mess over those who consider you mentors, even from afar, because they are looking to you as the example.

What influence are you leaving? As I walk through the doors of opportunities that allow me to connect with a myriad of Youth Leaders, I walk in with a confidential legacy because even at my age, my mother's teachings are so influential. I can hear her and feel her touch playing in the back of my head. Your experiences may feel relatively insignificant, but trust that they are influential. Take this knowledge and translate it into action! In Youth Ministry Leadership, your relationship with young people must be TRANSFORMATIONAL AND TRANSACTIONAL. Many scholars of leadership works would disagree, as *transactional leaders* usually operate solely to gain benefits from the ones who are producing.

However, in this framework, Youth leadership is artistic and designed to challenge your growth and ability to be introspective. Yes, there must be 100% self-evaluation so that you do not project on others your intimidation, your areas of lack, and your fears of change. Do you know what type of relationship you have with your youth and young adults? Is there a relationship that has been bought or genuinely earned?

Transformation, or the art of successfully connecting generations, forms a nation of warriors and leaders by gathering intel that allows you to productively guide the trajectory of young lives. Youth Ministry Leadership is an art; however, many who do not have the passion fail to perfect the craft. More than the occasional activities and the designated Sunday interactions, Youth Ministry must be embedded in passion.

When we speak about progressive youth ministry leadership, we must first identify what is STAGNANT. What are the apparent gaps? Where are the missing elements? How long have the pieces not been connected? What is absent, and where are the issues that need a solution?

If we are not careful, we will judge what we do not understand - and instead of matching efforts with resources and research, we will be the halt to progression that causes paralysis. We will continue to place a band-aid on areas needing surgical attention because we will become hidden in comfort.

LET S CONNECT!

Do me a favor. Grab a blank sheet of paper, a good writing pen, an accountability partner, and a great cup of coffee. Yes! You always have to be ready to work as a Youth Leader.

Now do this with me – for yourself – and the group of those you are leading. Take five minutes to describe your personality in writing. After you have completed that task, assess what you have written. With your paper turned down, ask your accountability partner to answer those questions with honesty. This requires vulnerability and openness to feedback. Would leaders and the young people around you say the same? Are the answers true to what others would say about you?

1. HOW DO I SHOW UP FOR YOUTH MINISTRY AS A YOUTH LEADER?

_____

_____

_____

2. WHO DO YOUNG PEOPLE SAY I AM?

_____

_____

_____

3. MIRROR CHECK: PERSONALITY PROFILE

GLOWS	GROWS
EXAMPLE: Outgoing	EXAMPLE: Self-Centered

THE MAGIC OF CONNECTION

onnection with young people and other Youth Leaders on your team is something that should NEVER be bought. It is the inevitable connection of understanding all sides of people and accepting, with prayer, their personalities, without gifts, tokens, fancy dinners, money, or compromise.

Young people are people. They smell distress. They are keen in their discernment of organization and are only impressed by actions. Young people are to be loved through actions and methods of discipleship that keep them on a straight and narrow path.

Many Youth Leaders have a hard time connecting with young people because they are afraid of those whom they are mentoring. Yes. Mentoring. Youth leaders are always on display and always being interviewed by young people, whether they ever speak to you or not.

Connection surpasses discipline. Connection involves relationships. Youth Leaders who fail to build relationships and issue words of discipline are almost always the ones that are not respected and often disobeyed. While being a Youth Leader is not about "making friends" with young people, it is about building friendships that invite trust and open communication.

In fact, if you are guilty of being the Youth Leader who trades incentives for relationships, it is time to re-evaluate your purpose and, further, your reason for wanting to be involved as a Youth Ministry Leader.

Youth Ministry is not about an enterprise of self-promotion or riding a wave to fulfill a personal agenda item vicariously. It is not about building *your* ministry *inside* of a ministry. It is not even about the position you have been appointed to serve.

Rather, it is about the people to whom you have been called. It is about the formation of a future and the careful development of the next generation. It is about establishing the Kingdom of God through a generation of young people who will grow under your tutelage and win souls to Christ.

So, you need to have on the right clothes! You need to have on the right armor, the right body suit, and the right gear. You need skating clothes when you are at the roller rink! Am I making myself clear?

FUN FACTS

Building better relationships and communicating more efficiently starts with KNOWING those around you. Take time to share fun facts about your personal likes and dislikes.

Share a list of hobbies, interests, foods, movies, shopping spots, restaurants, and even gas stations that are apart of who you are.

Take a moment to ask your group leaders their favorite colors, choice of ice-cream, or their preference of coffee versus tea. You will be surprised about the commonalities that are gained in this time of genuine collaboration.

LET'S REVIEW

- ❖ Connection is about creating great relationships with young people.
- ❖ The relationships you build in Youth Ministry Leadership will be tested by disagreements, fire, trials, and hard times.
- Relationships are about sharing in the dreams, hopes, goals, and lives of others and sacrificing yourself for the good of those whom you are leading.

When was the last time you treated your Youth Leaders for the hard work they have done? While this can be a bit tricky, seeing as how some Youth Leaders are not as developed, never exempt them from recognition and praise. The more valuable someone feels, the more involved they will become.

Be guilty of investing in people. There are so many ways you can invest in the forward trajectories of others. Be intentional and invest in others where it matters. This is known as "adding value."

Stop living through young people and start leading them!

CHAPTER

3

ARE YOU READY?

Youth Ministry is not glamourous – rewarding, but not glamourous. Youth Ministry is three hundred and sixty-five days a year! It happens around the clock, with sleeves up and hearts all in. It is a continual building of a community, as it truly "takes a village" to develop the lives of young people.

Many parts of Youth Ministry are planned; however, there are segments of Youth Ministry that are not. Young people cannot be "scheduled" in. They are NOT concerned about how smart you are, more than they are concerned about your consistency.

The issues they face are insurmountable, and YOU, the Youth Leader, MUST be equipped with the right heart and the proper gear to combat the challenges that will unquestionably strengthen your walk with God as you commune with Him in prayer on their behalf.

STOP for a moment. Ask yourself:

Is Youth Ministry **driving** me or **dragging** me?*Express Yourself.*

_____

_____

Do I have the**motivation** to sharpen my tools for Youth Ministry Leadership? *Express Yourself.*

_____

_____

Now be honest. As a Youth Leader: Are you FUN? Are you regarded as a leader? Are you exciting? Do people see you as a pushover? Are you STRICT? Are you  engaging? Are you boring and starchy? Do young people shy away from you like they do vegetables? Do young people genuinely like you as a person? Are you easy to get along with? Are young people automatically drawn to you? Are you a Youth Leader out of obligation? Are you passionate about young people and their success? How many young people are better because of you? Is the relationship young people have with God a result of your impact?

These are heavy questions, and your personality plays an essential role in the answers. The answers also, in turn, affect how you show up. Be honest with yourself, and where adjustments can be made, MAKE THEM!

How you SHOW UP is more important than what you put out. It is more important than what you say and more important than what you do. When young people feel connected, they are more likely to *respect* your role – get this – even if you are not really good *in* your role!

It is the truth. If anyone disagrees, call me, and let's chat about it! Believe me. There are plenty of Youth Leaders who are "feeling their way through." They are not equipped with the techniques, but they have mastered the art of **connection**.

You cannot be afraid to fight in prayer, and you cannot be afraid of research! With the talent you have in your Youth Ministry, refrain from trying to do everything! This leads to BURN OUT – Do you know what else leads to burnout? DOING ABSOLUTELY NOTHING!

If Youth Ministry is driving you from the inside and you are motivated to sharpen your skills and keep them crisp, I would venture to say that YOU ARE READY! Notice, I didn't say you were perfect. I didn't say you have or will have all the resources or the answers. But I did declare that **YOU ARE READY**! Ready for what, you ask?

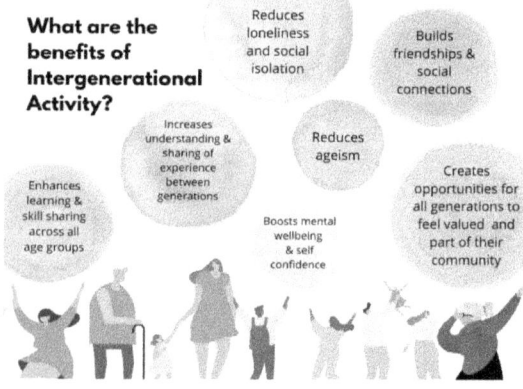

What are the benefits of Intergenerational Activity?

Reduces loneliness and social isolation

Builds friendships & social connections

Increases understanding & sharing of experience between generations

Reduces ageism

Enhances learning & skill sharing across all age groups

Boosts mental wellbeing & self confidence

Creates opportunities for all generations to feel valued and part of their community

New clothes. New armor. New information. New techniques. New tactics. New strategies. New connections. NEW! You are ready to move into a fresh perspective and tap into a new fountain that is refreshed by the love you have for God's little children.

For what it is worth, **CONFLICT** will meet you in the place to which you are **CALLED**. Therefore, the place of conflict is not the place to concede or compromise. Rather, it is the place to *connect, cultivate, and contend*. You are ready to become the village – the intercessor – the warrior – the bridge. Yes. You are ready to prepare a generation to carry the land to its next dimensional wave of Glory. You are ready.

CHAPTER

4

EQUIPPED TO FIT AND FLOW

S ince you are ready to show up, let me assure you that your readiness and how you show up determine how young people respond. It is like a mathematical equation. The factors that you bring to the table will ultimately produce a response. Check this equation. 1+1=2. It's that simple. That response either yields a negative or a positive charge.

Regardless of the response, Youth Leaders are responsible for setting the tone of the atmospheric equation and charging the zone so that it is conducive to an affirmative environment for every young person under your assignment umbrella.

While you may flow in a specified area of Youth Ministry, a Youth Ministry Leader must be agile enough to adapt to every phase of Youth Ministry to fit as a well-rounded Youth Ministry Leader. Every young person needs to be reassured that you are concerned about their plight and about who they are. Sure. I get it. I, too, only thought I was called to ages 18-25 until I became a Youth Ministry Director!

If you cannot BRIDGE, you cannot BUILD.

TAKEITHA PETERSON CARTER

I learned quickly that even though that age group acted as a jumper cable to my heart, I had to learn how to trigger that same care for the 4–6-year-olds. My fear of not really knowing how to relate to them perhaps was largely misguided by the deep-seated noise of people telling me that I was not fit to care for them because I was not a biological parent.

Indeed. Let's interject a piece of my transparent experience about not being a biological parent – but being called to the assignment of Youth Ministry. Well, I heard it all. It was painful, and hearing that my ability to connect with younger people was somehow debilitated by the fact that I was not raising one of them was as far from the truth as the east is from the west!

As I started working with them and building relationships with the younger children, as fervently as I was building them with my favorite age bracket of young adults, I found out something extraordinarily unique. The children were not concerned about the fact that I was not a biological parent because, to them, I became a sister, a friend, an aunt – their Youth Leader. I even became "the woman who shows up with a purse of candy!" I was the one that would become "their outlet," and they intrinsically knew that they could tell me anything – sometimes more than what I could handle.

My point is that fear and the deafening noise of people swiftly created a false insecurity that I had to learn to over-come IF I was going to lead young people. Further in this truth is the absolute idea that I was not only leading young people, but I was also leading the parents, the guardians, the grandparents, and the caretakers of this generation.

With that notion, let's just stay on this path. Remember the noise I just stated? Well, it was primarily coming from a group of parents – and other adults - who felt like I was not qualified to lead youth. Their thoughts were freely ex-pressed, burying me in a mound of shame that would cause me to freeze in leadership competencies. I mean, I had a dog who I took great care of, but that did not measure up to NOT being a biological parent.

So - I went to God about the "noise," and with tears, I began to tell Him that I really wanted to be a great Youth Leader, but I was not a parent. I told Him my barren woes, and in that instant, He whispered to me the most powerful and simultaneously comical statement. He said, "My daughter. I have called you for this work. I have designed your hands to carry this work. You are ingenious, and the creative flair you shall bring forth will be like nothing you have ever seen. Understand that having kids does not make you any more a Youth Leader than knowing a scripture makes you a preacher."

I heard this in my good ear, and my immediate response was, "Huh?" Insert a chuckle. Yep. I was baffled. Stunned, to say the least. It made so much sense. I thought about that statement from God, and I got myself up, dried my face, put the black paint under my eyes, rolled up my sleeves, and went to work.

ACTIVITY:
WHAT ARE THEY
SAYING?

Have an open forum for candid feedback. This allows you to "*hear*" what you cannot "*see*" as the leader. Height limits sight. In other words, the higher you are on the rung of leadership, the more distant you are from the ground. Therefore, your leadership perspective is skewed by what is reported versus what is realistic. Voices from the field open avenues for improvement.

ACTIVITY:
WHERE ARE THE
YOUNG PEOPLE?

Young people are on their devices! What are some holistic approaches to preparing youth for the outside world? How do we prepare them beyond the four walls of the church? Corporate America awaits them. They are in need of financial literacy. Young people depend on you for answers about college, dating, family dynamics, and balancing money, time, and fun. Evaluate methods of implementation.

5

QUALIFIED TO SERVE

There is an apparent truth: People will construct monuments of fear around you in hopes that the fear will get inside you, as their desire is for you to concede or fail. Once fear is inside you, it becomes a cancer of the mind and leprosy to your thoughts. Fear will overwhelm you to the point of convincing yourself that you are not good enough to lead and that maybe the "crowd" is right. But what did God say?

I knew His voice. I knew my mandate, and my only obligation was to obey. We get lost right here because we feel that we somehow owe people an in-depth explanation, putting us in a place of consistently trying to prove our worth and skills to people who will NEVER accept us, no matter how well we perform or how much we explain.

> **Never measure success by the number of activities presented; rather, measure success by the impact you have on individual relationships you constantly BUILD with young people.**
>
> TAKEITHA PETERSON CARTER

To me, my gift to God was my obedience to Him, and God had given me the green light. He lit within me a fire and a passion for young people that carried me beyond the four walls of the church - And when you plug the noise of fear and self-doubt, obeying God against all odds, your ministry with and for young people will take on a completely different trajectory.

ACTIVITY:
WHO ARE THESE PEOPLE?

Take a moment to identify those who fall into these generational categories. Once they are identified, what are ways you can leverage connection? Knowing the intergenerational groups you will interact with as a youth leader is important. Much research has been recorded to ensure that we are equipped to respond effectively to generational segments.

	Silent (1922-1945)	Boomer (1946-1964)	GenX (1965-1980)	GenY (1981-2000)
Work Ethic	Sacrifice	Workaholic	Self-Reliance	Multi-Task
Work is...	an obligation.	an adventure.	a challenge.	fulfillment.
Leadership Style	Directive	Consensual	No Layers	NOW
Interactive Style	Individual	Team Player	Entrepreneur	Participative
Communications	Written	Face to Face	Direct	Email
Rewards	Job well done	Money & Title	Freedom	Meaningful Work
Messages that Motivate	Your experience is respected	You are valued and needed	Do it your way	Work with bright, creative people.
Work & Family	Work	No balance	Balance	Balance

Questions to Ponder

1. What makes you most passionate about Youth Ministry?

_____

_____

_____

_____

_____

2. Do you believe that you are in the right season of Youth Ministry?

_____

_____

_____

_____

_____

3. Are you ministering to the proper age group?

_____

_____

_____

_____

_____

4. Are you relative and relatable?

_____

_____

_____

_____

_____

5. Do you complain about your Youth Ministry assignment or face it head-on with gladness?

_____

_____

_____

_____

_____

6. Have you taken an assessment to evaluate your personality within the last three years?

_____

_____

_____

_____

_____

7. Are you easily irritated by others?

_____

_____

_____

_____

_____

Young people will
not always need to
be informed, but
they will always need
to be invited.

TAKEITHA PETERSON CARTER

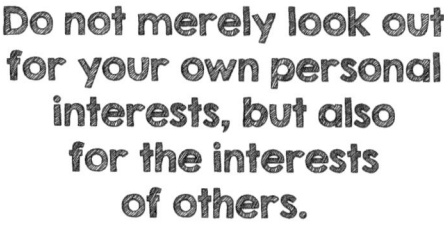

Do not merely look out
for your own personal
interests, but also
for the interests
of others.

PHILIPPIANS 2:4

ACTIVITY

Amongst a group of Youth Leaders, discuss at least five (5) creative times during the year you can reward young people outside of birthdays and graduation celebrations. Hint: Go beyond the four walls on this challenge to create five.

1.

2.

3.

4.

5.

VIRTUAL CONNECTION: ARE YOU LOST?

During the pandemic, many of us were introduced to new-found ways of connecting digitally. As we move past the pandemic, how has Youth Ministry engagement changed for you and your Youth Ministry team(s)? What types of plans have you made to safely incorporate in-person Youth Ministry activity models and ensure the longevity of the department? Have you connected with young people through hybrid means and set a cadence expectation of connection? There is a part of commitment that challenges us to climb and not quit. If there is a hunger to be connected virtually, INVEST in yourself by bringing young people into your sphere that can teach in the digital space. Allow them to operate as digital connectors, ambassadors of social media, and directors of technological advances that can help the ministry at large. LEVERAGE CAPACITY!

BTW: ALL excuses MUST be buried! There is not one excuse (except a good one) that would make you leave young people behind because of the territories that create opportunities for change. The breaking news is that NOTHING will be the same again – EVER! As leaders, we should be willing to adjust our sails quickly, especially with young lives at stake. Without YOUTH, you have no YOUTH MINISTRY.

THANK YOU always
gets the gold.

TAKEITHA PETERSON CARTER

WORKING THE NETWORK

1. Never operate from levels of intimidation. Instead, be instrumental in incorporating gifts and talents that lend to healthy, well-rounded youth entities which strengthen the organization at large. Every encounter is a time of preparation.

2. Go the extra mile *without* pay or praise and work AHEAD of schedule. Create activities and events in a timely fashion. Do not expect leaders, parents, and youth to jump as a result of your LACK of planning. Create schedules in advance and align them with the vision of the Senior Pastor.

3. Find VALUE. Focusing on complaints and negative aspects of the operation drags productivity. This means that you must trust those on the ground and in the field. High "flight" diminishes "sight." Therefore, while you sit at the top rung of the ladder, remember that team members are "on the ground" with insight that needs always to be considered, even if it is not incorporated.

4. Listen attentively and create a safe space that invites honesty, transparency, and vulnerability.

5. Always be approachable and unafraid to lean into different personalities.

6. Find the value in EVERY individual and be committed to developing it. Create the "THINK TANK" and invite them to have a seat at the table! Every brain needs to be in the game.

7. Everyone has an opinion. Strategically learn how to incorporate each voice without undermining or pushing aside people and their thoughts. Allow team leaders to THINK BEYOND RESOURCES! As ideas become identified, you will be surprised at the SOLUTIONS that sit amongst you.

8. Stop being afraid of social media! The digital highway is full of ways that increase visibility and efficiency. Make it work for the department, and it will enhance the work of the ministry at large.

9. Clean up the culture of the environment. Leaders who talk badly about youth and team members create a "dirty" culture. Never be accused of "splashing mud" on the culture of your group.

10. Tell the truth! Always be upfront and transparent with team leaders.

CHAPTER

HOW OLD ARE YOU?

Have you ever asked the question, "How old are you?" Well, if you have never asked, you've been asked, and I am almost sure you have sung this phrase at some point. Let me interject that this question is not just a piece of a birthday song. In fact, it is a question that every Youth Leader should ask within their sphere of Youth Leadership.

Statistically, culture changes every five years. However, in accordance with research, the culture of the church changes every twenty years. Yes. You read that correctly. EVERY 20 YEARS. It is amazing to me that Youth Ministry Leaders are lost in their attempts to connect with young people, but they are clearly ministering within a bracket of time that stifles relatability. If you are hearing phrases like, "That's so 20th century," or "We don't say that anymore," or "I have no clue what you just said," you definitely need to revolutionize your Youth Ministry swag and update your lingo!

For example, if I am in my 40s, as a Youth Ministry Leader, it will be a bit difficult for me to relate to a 15-year-old. It is not that I cannot *teach* the 15-year-old; however, I am more effective in teaching those who are generationally ready to embrace what I bring to the table. In my 40s, I am more relatable to someone in their mid-20s or early 30s.

The gaps in technology, education, and career paths are not as large, creating a more relatable conversation. I am regarded by this group as one they can look up to, respect, and at times, refer to as "big sis" or "auntie." To the 15-year-old, I am "mom" or, in some cases, "grandma."

Understanding the culture, the vernacular, and generational barriers help Youth Ministry Leaders connect more effectively. In this example, my assignment should include teaching financial literacy, helping young adults discover the paths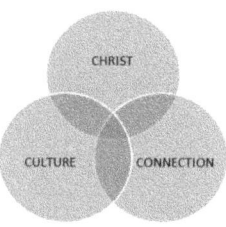
in life, and offering opportunities to showcase their talents while simultaneously adjoining conversations about building stable professions and maintaining healthy relationships.

As we evolve in Youth Ministry Leadership, we must be cognizant of WHO we are ministering to and ensure that our life lessons, which are foundational in Jesus Christ and His most Holy Word, are given to the group we have been called to. Let us not be irresponsible with our gifts. We must be careful not to cast our pearls to the swine or place our calling in an unsuitable category. RELEVANCE MATTERS!

POINT OF CONVERSATION: *How are you managing the relevance of culture against the standards of Christ in an effort to remain connected?*

Because of the unsuitable categories we are placed in relative to Youth Ministry, frustration becomes our biggest enemy. Once frustration cements, complaining follows. They walk hand in hand. Frustration and complaining are two peas in a pod. You will not get one without the other. They are best friends and an adversary in any mission!

MONTHLY TOPICS OF DISCUSSION

JANUARY	Generation Z: Dealing with Anxiety and Depression (Matthew 6:31-34)
FEBRUARY	I Am Loved by God (John 3:16; Romans 8:38-39)
MARCH	Building Friendships (Proverbs 17:9; Colossians 3:13)
APRIL	I Am Rooted in The Word of God (Psalm 90:12; Ephesians 5:15-17; James 4:14)
MAY	You Are the Light (Matthew 5:13; 14-16)
JUNE	Resisting the Bad Attitude (Ephesians 4:31-32)
JULY	Free from the Power of Sin (Luke 10:38-42)
AUGUST	Social Media and the Truth of Our Identity (1 Peter 2:9-10)
SEPTEMBER	*Special Youth & Parent Session / Overcoming Racial Bias*
OCTOBER	Living a Life of Integrity (Psalm 139:23-24)
NOVEMBER	Gratefulness (Luke 17:11-19)
DECEMBER	Defeat the Bully (Matthew 5:43-44)

Get comfortable realizing that as a Youth Leader, your voice matters and that young people want to hear from you when you are PREPARED! Trust me. Young people are keen, and they are aware when you lack topic skill, organization, and preparation, so always stay a few steps ahead.

Aside from biblical commentaries, what other materials can you utilize as resources to strengthen your presentations? Young people are not looking for "smart;" they are looking for relevance and foundational truths.

CHAPTER

7

PASSION OVER POSITION

Successful youth leaders are disciplinary figures who have first created a safe haven nestled in genuine relationships. Long after ingenuine people walk out of the lives of youth and young adults, those with a pure heart, a true commitment, and a desire to impart and prepare the next generation will yet be hanging strong. Young people trust those who are invested in their well-being to call out their wrongdoings and further trust them to celebrate them in doing things well. Youth Leaders who are authentically connected mold young people who never want to disappoint them – and when they do, they are deeply saddened and regretful.

As a Youth Ministry Leader, I have discovered that young people glean from every aspect of your life and positively mimic who they see. I have had opportunities to lead large groups of young people in my tenure as a Servant Youth Leader.

The joy of watching young people mature is only a reward understood by those who appreciate watching their hard work blossom. That journey of youth ministry leadership was more than a titled position – it became my greatest passion.

After a while, serving in Youth Ministry Leadership roles pushes you beyond the bright lights and "stage fright," no matter how large or small the ministry you serve in is. Early on, I had to grow a tough skin and learn to get over what others anticipated or perhaps even expected of me, as my primary mission was to transform a present generation - for future generations.

In my quest, I hit some hard detours and experienced unexpected crossroads. There were months when I felt like everything I did was for naught. It even seemed as though my time, resources, money, and desire to help were overshadowed by ungrateful

> **In the absence of resource, innovation and creativity is necessary You are not stuck where you START, you get stuck where you STOP.**
>
> TAKEITHA PETERSON CARTER

young people, lackadaisical youth workers, and worse, very mean parents! This is where I found out that there is such a thing as "comfortable discomfort."

It's time to lean into what feels uncomfortable for you as a Youth Ministry Leader. Say this with me: "FRESH AND NEW." Yes. Fresh and new. When you step out of your comfortable place, you find that there is a world of innovation and insight that awaits your grasp. You have to say no to the plateau. Remember the new car smell? That smell made you make promises to yourself that you wish you'd never broken. The smell made you promise never to eat in your car. That smell made you promise that the bottom of your shoes would never touch your floor mat because you would never remove the paper that covered it. The point here is that the smell of that new car allowed your mind to think outside of the norm. Your thoughts propelled promises, which in turn, created PROTECTION. You worked hard to maintain the freshness of what was new, and you also embraced untapped potential.

This combination of resistance, new, submission, and discomfort were enough for me to throw it all away and walk free, but something greater compelled me to remain steadfast to the call of the generation. No, it was not a bi-weekly check for my services. It was not the occasional rendering of praise for my hard work. It was not the pats on the back for being able to galvanize youth and motivate them to participate in activities. Rather, it was the *commission* of the *mission* , the call of passion, and the drive to see young people excel in their God-given potential. Here is where we learn that bends in the road are not dead ends to the road. These barriers test your drive and develop a passion.

I made a vow to God, and while in prayer one evening, with tears flowing down my face in a cry to God for help, He whispered to me: "Your **COMMITMENT** must override the **CRITICISM**." In that moment, I began to tell God "YES" and opened my heart to receive His care and guidance. I have taken the role of "Youth Leader" as seriously as a parent extends protection for their child. God knew the deep desire of my heart. And that desire to please Him in leading the generations has brought me to where I am now.

Youth Leaders, only what you do for Christ will last. PRAYER. PRAYER. PRAYER. Youth Leaders, PRAYER is the priority of leadership. It is the benchmark, the foundation, and the KEY to success in youth ministry. With all the issues we contend with, a private prayer life is how you care for yourself – and others. Seek God for answers on how to make real connections that are not rooted in fear but rather in faith.

Make sure that your position does not cloud the passion for young people. Remember that how you show up makes all the difference in how you create the magic of activities that become the bridge to relevant connections!